CW01506464

THE POCKET

Scottish English

Published in 2025
by Gemini Books
Part of Gemini Books Group

Based in Woodbridge and London
Marine House, Tide Mill Way
Woodbridge, Suffolk IP12 1AP
United Kingdom

www.geminibooks.com

Text and Design © 2025 Gemini Adult Books Ltd
Part of the Gemini Pockets series

Cover image: Shutterstock/Gulf GM

ISBN 978-1-78675-186-7

All rights reserved. No part of this publication may be reproduced in any
form or by any means – electronic, mechanical, photocopying, recording or
otherwise – or stored in any retrieval system of any nature without prior
written permission from the copyright holders.

A CIP catalogue record for this book is available from the British Library.

Disclaimer: The book is a guidebook purely for information and entertainment
purposes only. All trademarks, individual and company names, brand
names, registered names, quotations, celebrity names, logos, dialogues and
catchphrases used or cited in this book are the property of their respective
owners. The publisher does not assume and hereby disclaims any liability to
any party for any loss, damage or disruption caused by errors or omissions,
whether such errors or omissions result from negligence, accident or any other
cause. This book is an unofficial and unauthorized publication by Gemini Adult
Books Ltd and has not been licensed, approved, sponsored or endorsed by any
person or entity.

Printed in China

10 9 8 7 6 5 4 3 2 1

THE
POCKET

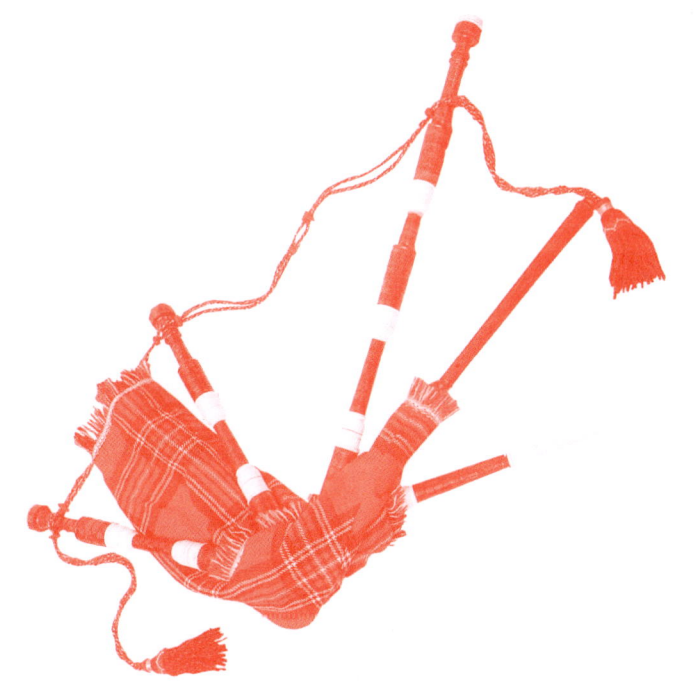

Scottish
English

G:

Contents

Introduction

This excellent beginner's guide to the uniquely colourful English spoken in Scotland includes Scottish slang and idioms, many derived from Scottish Gaelic. Filled with everyday phrases, compliments and even insults, it will help you to know your 'Arbroath smokies' from your 'wynds', your 'trews' from your 'sporran', and ... 'lang may yer lum reek'! Revealing, entertaining and amusing, this is a handy pocket guide for any visitor to Scotland.

Some say that Scots use more slang than English, but whether that's true or not, the speech of most Scots is certainly peppered with slang. So, whether you're visiting 'Glesga' (Glasgow), home to 'Weegies', short for Glaswegians, the Granite City (Aberdeen) or the capital – known as 'Auld Reekie' for the same reason that London was once and sometimes still is known as the 'Big Smoke' – this concise guide will come in handy.

There are many old Scottish sayings dating back to our grandparents' day and beyond, but there are also many fairly recent inventions. Some of the older ones are rarely used now, which may be just as well, as they may

baffle even a Scot, particularly depending on which part of Scotland you're in.

Scottish English varies greatly from the Highlands to South Ayrshire and from the east of the country to the west, with different words sometimes being used to describe the same thing in different places.

Some sayings will 'make yer heid mince', some are poetic and many will just make you laugh. This is a book for visitors to Scotland and for anyone crossing the border, in either direction. It will also evoke a pang of homesickness in any Scottish expatriate.

While a concise guide can't possibly be exhaustive, it can, as this handy pocket book does, offer a revealing and entertaining selection of words and idioms in common usage.

SCOTTISH

–

ENGLISH

A

A

SCOTTISH	ENGLISH
a'	all
a'body	anybody
aboot	about
advocate	barrister
ae	indicates agreement – 'She's coming wi' us, ae?'
aff	off
ah	I
airt	direction, quarter point of compass
ashet	large plate for meat
auld	old
auld lang syne	days of long ago
Auld Reekie	Edinburgh
awfy	awfully, very
aye	yes, always

Arbroath smokie

haddock smoked to a rich copper colour

'Arbroath smokies' were awarded PGI
(Protected Geographical Indication) status
in 2004, so can be produced only within a
five-mile radius of the town centre. Using
traditional methods dating back to the late
1800s, haddock from the cold North Sea are
tied in pairs on wooden sticks and smoked
three feet above a fire in a brick 'barrel' for
thirty to forty-five minutes. The result is golden
brown on the outside with creamy, firm flesh
inside – slightly smoky, almost sweet.

B

B

SCOTTISH	ENGLISH
baffies	slippers
bahoochie, also **behouchie**	buttocks
baillie	magistrate
bairn	child
Balmoral	flat, round bonnet
bampot	idiot
bannock	thick oatmeal cake
bap	bread roll
barkit	dirty
barra	small child
bastart	bastard, also a term of endearment
batter	**to** beat up
bawbag	scrotum, also a term of abuse

SCOTTISH	ENGLISH
bawheid	a stupid person
baws	testicles
beadle	verger
bejant	first-year undergraduate (St Andrew's and Aberdeen)
ben	mountain
besom	broom
bez	beer
bide	to stay, live
biggin	building, cottage
big yin	term of endearment for older relatives or friends, literally 'big one', also, capped up, an affectionate nickname for comedian Billy Connolly
birk	birch tree

B

SCOTTISH	ENGLISH
birl (*v.*)	spin round
black bun	spiced fruit loaf eaten at New Year

bramble

blackberry

According to the *Dictionaries of the Scots Language,* as well as being known as brambles in Scotland, the blackberry, *Rubus fruticosus,* has also been known as a 'bumblekite', a 'blackbide' and a 'scaldberry'.

SCOTTISH	ENGLISH
blate	slow, backward, shy
blether (*n.* and *v.*)	a chatterbox, also to talk nonsense
blootered	very drunk
boak	a dry heave, an expression of disgust
boggin'	smelly, dirty
bolt	to go away
bonny, also **bonnie**	pretty, handsome
bosie	bosom, a cuddle
bothy	farm cottage
bourtree	elder tree
bowfin'	sick-making
brae	hill

B

SCOTTISH	ENGLISH
brammer	a term of endearment
braw	good-looking, beautiful, really nice
breeks	trousers
brig	bridge
broon	brown
bubbly-jock	turkey
Bucky	Buckfast, a tonic wine popular in Scotland
buits	boots
burd	girl, or girlfriend
burn	small river or stream
buttery	type of breakfast roll
byre	cowshed

bonspiel

curling match

A match between two clubs or parishes. Originally, this could have applied to golf or archery too. The first clubs were formed in Scotland, and Scottish emigrants took the game to Canada, the United States, New Zealand and elsewhere. Also known as the 'roarin' game', from the noise of the granite stone on the ice, curling is one of the world's oldest team sports.

C

SCOTTISH	ENGLISH
cairn	heap of stones marking a spot or path
cannae	cannot
canny	smart, also wary, careful
cauld	cold
ceilidh (pron. *kaylay*)	informal evening of song and story
champit tatties	mashed potatoes
chib	to stab, headbutt
chitter (*v.*)	shiver
chug	to masturbate
chum	to go with someone
clachan	small village
claes	clothes
clamjamphrie	mob, rabble
clan	social group sharing the same surname

SCOTTISH	ENGLISH
clart	to spread thickly
clarted	thickly covered
clarty, also clatty	dirty, muddy
cludgie	a toilet

clapshot

boiled turnips and potatoes mashed together

'Clapshot' was eaten originally in Orkney. Often served with haggis or oatcakes, sometimes swedes are used instead of turnips. The dish may also include some combination of chives, butter, dripping, cream or pepper, and some versions include onions.

SCOTTISH	ENGLISH
clype	a tell-tale
cookie	a plain bun
corbie	raven
Court of Session	the supreme civil court, in Edinburgh
couthie	agreeable
cowk	to retch, throw up
crabbit	bad-tempered, grumpy
creeshie	greasy
crivens	exclamation of surprise
croft	smallholding
cuddy	donkey or ass, a stubborn person

coble

small, flat-bottomed boat used for fishing

A traditional 'coble' is flat-bottomed, to allow launching from and landing on shallow, sandy beaches on Britain's east coast, and high-bowed to sail in the North Sea. A Scottish version, shallower and broader, is used for salmon-fishing off Arbroath and Montrose. Ghillies use a smaller version for fly fishing on Scottish rivers.

D

D

SCOTTISH	ENGLISH
da	dad
deave	deafen
defender	defendant
deid	very ('deid guid'), also dead
didnae	didn't
ding	hit, deal a blow
dinnae	don't
dirl	to shake, cause to vibrate
doo	pigeon
doocot	dovecot
doon	down
doonhamer	a person from Dumfries

SCOTTISH	ENGLISH
Doric	a Scottish dialect spoken in the north-east
douce	sedate, sober, quiet
doup	backside, bottom
dour	hard, obstinate, grim
dram	a drink, especially of whisky
dreich	damp, overcast, wet
dross	coal-dust
drouthy	dry, wanting rain, thirsty
dug	dog
dunderheid	idiot, fool
dunt	nudge, also thump, bump
durk	Highland dagger
dwam	swoon

Edina, also Embra

Edinburgh

Edinburgh Castle, built on a volcanic rock, is home to Scotland's crown jewels and the Stone of Destiny. It rises above the city that has been Scotland's capital since at least the fifteenth century. Edinburgh itself comprises a medieval Old Town and a Georgian New Town. Its original university, the University of Edinburgh, was founded in 1582.

SCOTTISH	ENGLISH
Eccie, Eccies	Ecstasy (the drug)
eejit	idiot
elder	office bearer in Presbyterian church
erse	arse
ettle (*v.*)	intend
factor	manager of estate, steward
fannybaws	a term of ridicule, sometimes endearment
fash (*n.* and *v.*)	trouble, annoy
feart	scared
feartie	coward

E F

SCOTTISH	ENGLISH
ferntickles	freckles
finnan haddie	cold-smoked haddock
firth	estuary
fitba'	football
fit like?	how are you? (Doric dialect)
flesher	butcher
flichterin'	soft fluttering, like the wings of a butterfly or a candle flame
flype	to turn partly inside out, e.g., a sock
foost	to become or smell mouldy
forby	besides
forenuin	morning
forrit	forward
frae	from

SCOTTISH	ENGLISH
fu'	drunk (full, of alcohol)
fud	the tail of a rabbit, the bottom, a term of abuse

finnock

young sea-trout

'Finnock' is the name given to small sea trout in their first year after smolt migration, during which the young fish (the smolt) begin to adapt to salt water, a process known as smoltification. Also knows as 'whitling', 'herling', 'school peal' and 'harvester', they are often found in estuaries or downstream in rivers.

SCOTTISH	ENGLISH
gad	exclamation of disgust (south-west)
gan, also **gang**	go

ginger

any flavour of fizzy soft drink

While a 'ginger' could be any flavour of soft drink, often it is 'Scotland's other national drink', Irn-Bru. Originally produced as Iron Brew in 1901, it is still made by A. G. Barr of Glasgow. Fizzy, bright orange, sweet and tangy, its recipe – said to include girders – remains a secret.

SCOTTISH	ENGLISH
gate	street
gey	good-sized, excellent
ghillie	sportsman's attendant
gigot	leg of mutton
gin	if
girdle	griddle
girn	grimace
glaikit	stupid, foolish
gleg	alert
glen	valley
glengarry	forage cap with a ribbon hanging down behind
Glesca, also Glesgae	Glasgow

G

SCOTTISH	ENGLISH
gloamin	twilight, dusk
gowk	fool, simpleton
granda	grandfather
grannied	well beaten in sport
greet	cry, weep
groond	ground
guid	good
guiser	a person in disguise, a mummer
gutties	gym shoes (gutta-percha is the tree sap from which rubber was made)
gyte	daft, crazy

gowan

a daisy, also other wildflowers

'Gowan' is the name used for various yellow or white wild flowers with a yellow centre, *Ranunculi* such as the buttercup or meadow crowfoot. A white gowan is an ox-eye daisy, but simply a gowan is generally taken to mean the common daisy, *Bellis perennis.*

H

SCOTTISH	ENGLISH
haar	a sea-mist off the North Sea
hame	home
haud	hold, stop
hauf	a half measure, usually of whisky
hauf an' hauf	a half measure of whisky and half a pint of beer
haugh	water meadow
haun	hand
haver	to speak nonsense, babble
haw	an expression like 'hey' or 'oi' to get someone's attention
heid	head
hen	term of endearment for a woman
herd	shepherd

SCOTTISH	ENGLISH
High Court of Judiciary	the supreme criminal court, in Edinburgh and circuit towns
Highers	Scottish School Leaving Certificate
hochmagandy	sex
Hogmanay	New Year's Eve
hoolet	owl
hoose	house
hoot	an exclamation of annoyance
howf	meeting place
howfin'	smelly
howk (*v.*)	dig
huddy-wuddy	in great excitement, confusion
hurl (*v.*)	wheel along, ride in a car or bus, etc.

I J

SCOTTISH	ENGLISH
ilk	of the same name, e.g., Guthrie of that ilk, i.e., Guthrie of Guthrie
ilka	each, every
interval	a period between morning and afternoon church services
isnae	isn't
jaked	drunk
jakey	tramp, drug addict
jalouse (*v.*)	to suspect
Jambo	a supporter of Heart of Midlothian Football Club (from the rhyming slang of jam tarts for Hearts)
jamp	jumped (Highlands, especially the Black Isle)

SCOTTISH	ENGLISH
janny	janitor
jessie	a wimp
jings	a mild expletive
jobby	a poo
jotter	exercise book

jobby-catchers

tracksuit bottoms

Just as some pubs used to show 'no shirt,
no shoes, no service' signs, a pub in Leith
has recently banned 'jobby-catchers', 'joggers'
with cuffed bottoms (some regard 'jobby-
catchers' to mean a two-piece tracksuit).
The same pub also banned 'mankles',
men's bare ankles.

K

K

SCOTTISH	ENGLISH
keech	shit, also nonsense
keek (*v.*)	peep, look
ken (*v.*)	know
kilt	Highland clothing for men, resembling a skirt, deeply pleated on the back and sides, from waist to knee, made of tartan cloth
kip (*n.* and *v.*)	a nap, to sleep
kippie	left-handed
kirk	church
kist	chest, coffin
knapdarloch	piece of poo hanging from an animal's fur or wool
kye	cows, cattle

kelpie

a mythical water demon resembling a horse

In Scottish folklore, a 'kelpie', or 'water kelpie', is a shape-shifting spirit which lives in a loch. Kelpies are usually described as resembling either grey or white horses, but they are able to adopt human form. *The Kelpies* are two thirty-metre-tall scuptures by the side of the M9 motorway between Falkirk and Grangemouth; they mark the point where the Forth and Clyde Canal meets the River Carron.

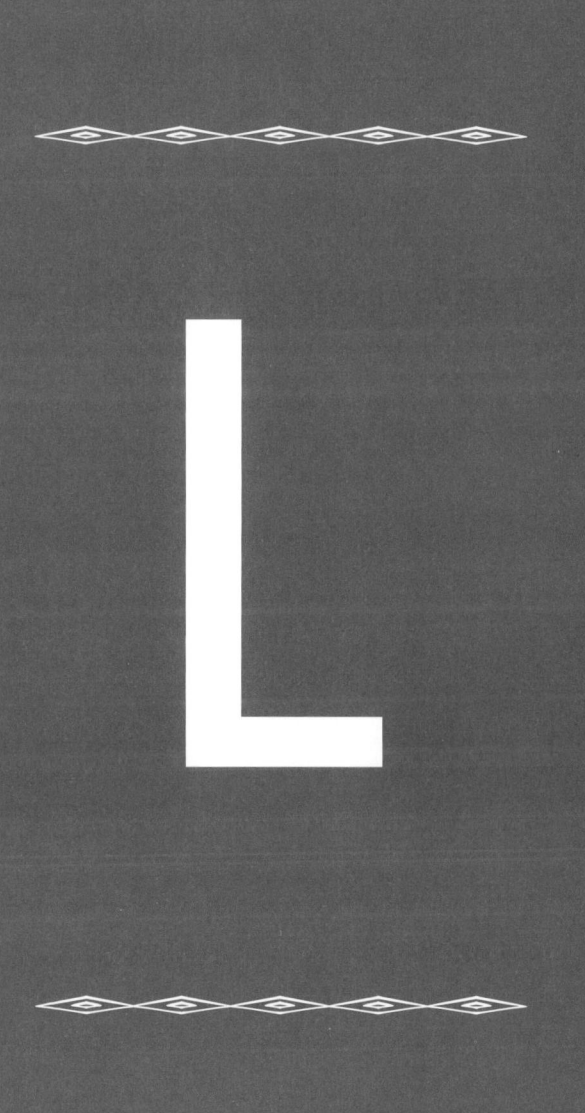

L

SCOTTISH	ENGLISH
laddie	a boy or young man
lade	water channel carrying water to a mill, a mill-race
laigh, also laich	low
laird	lord of the manor, squire
laldy	a thrashing, punishment
lamped	punched
lang-shankit	long-legged
lassie	girl
lavvy heid	toilet-head, literally 'lavatory-head' (insult)
lecky	electricity – 'Ah didnae pay me lecky this month'
links	golf course by the sea
loch	lake
loon	rogue, rascal
Lord Lyon	Chief Herald of Scotland

SCOTTISH	ENGLISH
lug	ear
Lyon Court	Scottish College of Arms

lum

chimney

'Lang may yer lum reek' which means 'long may your chimney smoke' is a classic Hogmanay greeting to wish someone a long, prosperous and comfortable life. The response, said to have originated in Edinburgh, is sometimes, 'Wi' ither folks' coal!' (with other people's coal), in other words, may you have an easy life, always provided for.

SCOTTISH	ENGLISH
mad wae it	very drunk indeed
mair	more
maist	most
manse	vicarage
maw	mum
melted	high (on drugs)
mibbe	maybe
mince	nonsense
mind (*v.*)	remember
mink	unhygienic person
mirk	dark
monadh	hill pasture

SCOTTISH	ENGLISH
moss	marsh, bog
muckle, also **meikle**	big
muir	moor

mask the tea

brew, or make, the tea

One meaning of 'mask' is to make wort for ale by mixing malt with hot water, in other words, to brew. Mask is also used to describe the process of infusing, or brewing, tea.

N

N

SCOTTISH	ENGLISH
nae danger	no chance
napper	head
naw	no
neb	nose
ned	hooligan, troublemaker
neebur	neighbour
neep	turnip
Ne'erday	New Year's Day
nicht	night
nip	kiss, also a single measure of spirits
nippin'	stinging
nippit	tight-fitting
nippy	sharp-tongued person, also spicy food
noo	now

nyaff

the talk of a child, the yelp of a small dog

In addition to describing the babbling of a young child or the yapping of a small dog, 'nyaff' has various figurative meanings, namely, to harp on about something, to talk in a senseless or frivolous way, or to argue snappishly.

P

Q

SCOTTISH	ENGLISH
och!	an exclamation of exasperation
oorie	dismal, gloomy
oot	out
oot yer nut	very drunk
orra	odd
orraman	farm labourer, odd-job man
ory	vulgar, common (Dundee)
outwith	outside, beyond
oxter	armpit
pal aboot wi	hang out with someone
pan breid	dead
park	field
partan	common edible crab

SCOTTISH	ENGLISH
patch	ignore someone, stand them up, not respond to their messages
patter	banter
pawkies	mittens
pawky	wily, sly, cunning
peedie	small
peely-wally	pale, wan, out of sorts
peevers	hopscotch
pend	arch, vault
period (*punctuation*)	full stop
piece	sandwich
pimps	easy
pinky, or pinkie	little finger
pish	bad, literally 'piss'
pizza crunch	pizza deep-fried in batter

O P Q

SCOTTISH	ENGLISH
plaid	rectangular length of twilled woollen cloth, often tartan, worn as an outer garment
poke	paper bag
pooched	broken, useless (Angus and Fife)
poond (*n.*)	pound
pouch	pocket
procurator fiscal	public prosecutor
provost, Lord Provost	mayor, Lord Mayor
puckle	a grain, granule
puddock	frog
punny eccy	punishment exercise at school
pure	very, totally
pursuer	plaintiff

SCOTTISH	ENGLISH
quaich	shallow drinking cup with two ears
quality	great, excellent
quean	young, unmarried woman

pibroch

form of bagpipe music – variations on a theme

A theme is first stated in a slow movement called a ground, or, in Scottish Gaelic, an *ùrlar*. The player then develops and embellishes the theme over the insistent harmony of the pipes' drones. 'Pibroch' is taken from *pìobaireachd*, which refers to piping in general. Unlike marches, jigs, reels and so on, pibroch can only be played on a set of pipes with its chanter, to play the melody, and its three drones, to provide the accompaniment.

R

R

SCOTTISH	ENGLISH
radge	crazy, angry
rat-arsed	drunk
rector	headmaster of academy, vicar in the Episcopal church, students' elected representative on university court
reek	smoke
reekie	smoky
reid	red
roaster	someone who is making a complete fool of themself
rocket	crazy or annoying person
rone, rhone	rainwater gutter
roup (*n.* and *v.*) (pron. *rowp*)	auction

reiver

sheep or cattle stealer

'Reivers' were active on the lawless frontier between then sovereign England and Scotland from the fourteenth to the late seventeenth centuries, when cattle rustling and other forms of disorder were common. Near constant warfare between the two countries offered little incentive to farmers, so plundering livestock became the major occupation. Scots were as likely to raid other Scots as the English; the two nationalities would occasionally even join forces. Reivers rode sturdy ponies known as 'hobblers'; their preferred weapon was the 'lang spear', or border lance.

S

S

SCOTTISH	ENGLISH
sair	sore
sannies	shoes, typically for sport
saorsa	freedom, liberty
Sassenach	English, English-speaking, formerly also applied to Lowlanders
scabby	dirty
scaffie	bin man
scrammle (*n.*)	scatter of coins or sweets to children at a wedding
scunner (*n.* and *v.*)	a nuisance, to sicken, disgust
scunnered	fed up, exhausted
sept	branch of clan with a different surname
sett	pattern of tartan
sgian dhu	a durk (dagger) worn in the stocking

SCOTTISH	ENGLISH
shak, shoggle	shake
shan	of poor quality
sheriff-clerk	registrar of sheriff court
sheriff-court	approximates to English county court, but also has wide criminal jurisdiction
sheriff-officer	bailiff, tipstaff
shilpit	thin, emaciated
shinty	game like hockey played in the Highlands
skelly-eyed	squint-eyed
skelp (*v.*)	slap, hit
skirl	shriek, sing shrilly, e.g., bagpipes
skreich	shriek, scream
skreich of day	daybreak, cockcrow

S

SCOTTISH	ENGLISH
slaister	make a mess
sleekit	ingratiating
slider	ice cream between wafers

spurtle

a pot-stick used for stirring porridge

This wooden kitchen tool, used to stir porridge, soups and stews, dates back to the fifteenth century. It creates less drag that a spoon, and porridge is less likely to stick to it. 'Spurtles' are commonly made from beech, cherry or maple wood, and often have a stylised thistle as a decorative element, as shown. Traditionally, a spurtle is stirred in a clockwise direction using the right hand.

SCOTTISH	ENGLISH
slitter (*v.*)	to dribble while eating
smirr	fine rain, drizzle
smuirich (*v.*)	to kiss
snashters	sweets, cakes, pastries
sneck	door catch
snib (*v.*)	to restrain, rebuke
solasta	luminous, shining
sort (*v.*)	mend
souk	a big softy
souter	shoemaker
square go	fair fight
stay	live – 'Where do you stay?'
stoater	someone or something which is fantastic

S

SCOTTISH	ENGLISH
stoor	to look glum
stot	a stupid, clumsy person
stovies	stewed potatoes and other ingredients
strath	valley, plain beside river
stravaig	to roam, wander
swage	to sit at the table waiting until one is able to eat some more
swally (*n.* and *v.*)	a drink, to swallow
swatch (*n.*)	a glimpse
swick (*n.* and *v.*)	a cheat, to cheat

sporran

ornamental pouch worn in front of kilt

The 'sporran', a leather purse or pouch, used to contain money and other small items, is a traditional part of Highland men's clothing, usually worn only for weddings and other special occasions. Sporrans are often highly ornamented with goat-hair, fur or metalwork, which commonly features Celtic designs.

T

T

tam-o'-shanter

*a soft woollen bonnet with a flat circular crown,
about twice as wide as the head*

The name of this traditional Scottish bonnet
for men is derived from 'Tam o' Shanter',
Robert Burns's long, narrative poem about
its eponymous hero, written in 1790, while
the poet was living in Dumfries. Similar to
the various flat bonnets common throughout
north-western Europe during the sixteenth
century, the 'tam-o'-shanter' is distinguished
by the decorative woollen ball, or 'toorie', in the
centre of its crown.

SCOTTISH	ENGLISH
tad (*adj.*)	a bit
tae	to, too
taps-aff	sunny weather ('tops off')
tapsalteerie	upside down, topy-turvy
tartan	woollen cloth woven in stripes of varying width and colour, repeated at regular intervals and crossing a similar set of stripes at right angles to form a pattern
tassie	a cup (for whisky)
tattie howker	potato picker
tatties	potatoes
teuchter	a Highlander (derogatory)
thole	to suffer, undergo
thrang	a large number
thrapple	throat

T

SCOTTISH	ENGLISH
toaty	small, tiny
tolbooth	old town hall (often with prison)
tollie	a poo
toonser	someone who lives in a city
trauchle (*v.*)	to trail, drag
trauchled (*adj.*)	tired and bothered
trews	close-fitting trousers of tartan cloth
troosers	trousers
tube	idiot
tup (*n.*)	a ram
turadh	a break in the clouds between rain showers
twa	two

tattie-bogle

a scarecrow, a simpleton

A 'bogle' is a ghost or spectre; a 'tattie-bogle',
a scarecrow set among growing potatoes. The
word's secondary meaning, a simpleton, is easy
enough to grasp.

W
Y

SCOTTISH	ENGLISH
wabbit	exhausted
wallap	to beat, thrash
waur	worse
wean	child, the youngest member of a family ('wee ane' – little one)
wee	small
wee barra	term of endearment, usually for boys, literally a 'small, fair-haired child'
wee yin	a younger or shorter person
whae	who
whaup	a curlew
wheen	a few
wheesht	be quiet
whigmaleerie	trinket, knick-knack

SCOTTISH	ENGLISH
winnae	will not
wisnae	was not
wouldnae	would not
wull	will
wynd	a narrow street, lane or alley
yak	eye
yaldi	an expression of excitement, joy
ye	you
yer	your
yett	gate, of a garden, field, etc.
yin	one
yonks	a long time

ENGLISH

–

SCOTTISH

A

ENGLISH	SCOTTISH
about	aboot
agreeable	couthie
alert	gleg
all	a'
angry	radge
annoy (*v.*)	fash
anybody	a'body
arch	pend
armpit	oxter
arse	erse
ass	cuddy
auction (*n.* and *v.*)	roup (*pron. rowp*)
awfully	awfy

B

ENGLISH	SCOTTISH
babble	haver
backside	doup
backward	blate
bad	pish
bad-tempered	crabbit
bagpipe music, variations on a theme	pibroch
bailiff	sheriff-officer
banter	patter
barrister	advocate
bastard	bastart
be quiet	wheesht
beat	wallap
beat up	batter
beautiful	bonny, bonnie, braw
become mouldy	foost
beer	bez
behind	bahoochie, behouchie
beyond	outwith
big	muckle, also meikle

big softy	souk
Billy Connolly	Big Yin
bin man	scaffie
birch tree	birk
bit	tad (*adj.*)
blackberry	bramble
bog	moss
boiled turnips and potatoes mashed together	clapshot
bonnet (flat, round)	Balmoral
boots	buits
bosom	bosie
bottom	doup, fud
branch of clan with a different surname	sept
bread roll	bap
break in the clouds between rain showers	turadh
breakfast roll	buttery
brew, or make, the tea	mask the tea
bridge	brig
broom	besom
brown	broon
Buckfast tonic wine	Bucky
bump	dunt
butcher	flesher
buttocks	bahoochie, behouchie

ENGLISH	SCOTTISH
cakes	snashters
cannot	cannae
careful	canny
cattle	kye
cause to vibrate	dirl
chatterbox	blether (*n.*)
cheat	swick (*n.* and *v.*)
chest	kist
Chief Herald of Scotland	Lord Lyon
child	bairn, wean
chimney	lum
church	kirk
close-fitting trousers of tartan cloth	trews
clothes	claes
coffin	kist
cold	cauld
cold-smoked haddock	finnan haddie
common	ory
common edible crab	partan

court, like an English county court	sheriff-court
coward	feartie
cows	kye
cowshed	byre
crazy	gyte, radge
crazy or annoying person	rocket
cry	greet
cuddle	bosie
cunning	pawky
cup (for whisky)	tassie
curlew	whaup
curling match	bonspiel

ENGLISH	SCOTTISH
dad	da
daft	gyte
daisy	gowan
damp	dreich
dark	mirk

days of long ago	auld lang syne
dead	deid, pan breid
deafen	deave
deal a blow	ding
defendant	defender
didn't	didnae
dig	howk
direction, quarter point of compass	airt
dirty	barkit, boggin', clarty, scabby
disgust	scunner (*n.* and *v.*)
dismal	oorie
donkey	cuddy
door catch	sneck
dovecot	doocot
down	doon
drag	trauchle (*v.*)
dribble while eating	slitter
drink (*n.*)	swally
drink (especially of whisky)	dram
drizzle	smirr
drug addict	jakey
drunk	fu', jaked, rat-arsed
drunk (very)	blootered, oot yer nut, mad wae it

dry	drouthy
dry heave	boak
durk (dagger, worn in the stocking)	*sgian dhu*
dusk	gloamin

ENGLISH	SCOTTISH
each	ilka
ear	lug
easy	pimps
Edinburgh	Auld Reekie, Edina, Embra
elder tree	bourtree
electricity	lecky
emaciated	shilpit
English, English-speaking	Sassenach
estuary	firth
every	ilka
excellent	gey, quality
exclamation of annoyance	hoot
exclamation of disgust	gad, boak
exclamation of exasperation	och!
exercise book	jotter
exhausted	scunnered, wabbit

expression like 'hey'	haw
expression of excitement or joy	yaldi
eye	yak

F

ENGLISH	SCOTTISH
fair fight	square go
farm cottage	bothy
farm labourer	orraman
fed up	scunnered
few	wheen
field	park
fine rain	smirr
first-year student (St Andrew's and Aberdeen)	bejant
fizzy soft drink (any flavour)	ginger
fool	gowk, dunderheid
foolish	glaikit
football	fitba'
forage cap	glengarry
forward	forrit
freckles	ferntickles
freedom	saorsa

frog	puddock
from	frae
full stop	period

| **ENGLISH** | **SCOTTISH** |

game like hockey played in the Highlands	shinty
gate (of a garden, field, etc.)	yett
girl	burd, lassie
girlfriend	burd
Glasgow	Glesca, Glesgae
glimpse (*n.*)	swatch
gloomy	oorie
go	gan, gang
go away	bolt
go with someone	chum
golf course by the sea	links
good	guid
good-looking	braw
good-sized	gey
grain	puckle
grandfather	granda
granule	puckle

greasy	creeshie
great	quality
griddle	girdle
grimace	girn
grumpy	crabbit

ENGLISH	SCOTTISH

half measure of whisky and half a pint of beer	hauf an' hauf
hand	haun
hang out with someone	pal aboot wi
head	heid, napper
headbutt	chib
headmaster of academy	rector
heap of stones marking a spot or path	cairn
high (on drugs)	melted
Highland clothing for men, resembling a skirt	kilt
Highland dagger	durk
Highlander (derogatory)	teuchter
hill	brae
hill pasture	monadh

hit	ding, skelp
hold	haud
home	hame
hooligan	ned
hopscotch	peevers
house	hoose
how are you?	fit like?

ENGLISH / SCOTTISH

ice cream between wafers	slider
idiot	bampot, dunderheid, eejit, tube
if	gin
ignore someone	patch
in great confusion or excitement	huddy-wuddy
indicates agreement	ae
informal evening of song and story	ceilidh
intend	ettle
isn't	isnae

J

ENGLISH	SCOTTISH
janitor	janny
jumped	jamp

K

ENGLISH	SCOTTISH
kiss	nip
kiss (*v.*)	smuirich
knick-knack	whigmaleerie
know	ken

L

ENGLISH	SCOTTISH
lake	loch
large number	thrang

large plate for meat	ashet
left-handed	kippie
leg of mutton	gigot
liberty	saorsa
little finger	pinky, pinkie
live	bide, stay
long time	yonks
look (*v.*)	keek
look glum	stoor
lord (of the manor)	laird
Lord Mayor	Lord Provost
low	laigh, laich
luminous	solasta

ENGLISH	SCOTTISH
manager (of estate)	factor
marsh	moss
mashed potatoes	champit tatties
masturbate	chug
maybe	mibbe
mayor	provost
meeting place	howf
mend	sort

mild expletive	jings
mill-race	lade
mittens	pawkies
mob	clamjamphrie
moor	muir
more	mair
morning	forenuin
most	maist
mountain	ben
muddy	clatty
mum	maw
mummer	guiser
mythical water demon resembling a horse	kelpie

N

ENGLISH	SCOTTISH
nap	kip
narrow alley, lane or street	wynd
neighbour	neebur
New Year's Day	Ne'erday
New Year's Eve	Hogmanay
night	nicht

no	naw
no chance	nae danger
nonsense	keech, mince
nose	neb
not respond to someone's messages	patch
now	noo
nudge	dunt
nuisance	scunner

ENGLISH	SCOTTISH
odd	orra
odd-job man	orraman
of poor quality	shan
of the same name	ilk
off	aff
office bearer in Presbyterian church	elder
old	auld
old town hall	tolbooth
one	yin, ane
ornamental pouch worn in front of kilt	sporran

out	oot
out of sorts	peely-wally
outside	outwith
overcast	dreich
owl	hoolet

P Q

ENGLISH	SCOTTISH
pale	peely-wally
paper bag	poke
pastries	snashters
pattern of tartan	sett
peep (*v.*)	keek
period between morning and afternoon church services	interval
person from Dumfries	doonhamer
person in disguise	guiser
pigeon	doo
pizza deep-fried in batter	pizza crunch
plain beside river	strath
plain bun	cookie
plaintiff	pursuer

pocket	pouch
poo	jobby, tollie
potato picker	tattie howker
potatoes	tatties
public prosecutor	procurator fiscal
punched	lamped
punishment	laldy
punishment exercise at school	punny eccy
quiet	douce

R

ENGLISH	**SCOTTISH**
rabble	clamjamphrie
rainwater gutter	rone, rhone
ram	tup (*n.*)
rascal	loon
raven	corbie
really nice	braw
rebuke (*v.*)	snib

rectangular length of twilled woollen cloth, often tartan	plaid
red	reid
registrar of sheriff court	sheriff-clerk
remember	mind
restrain	snib
retch	cowk
ride in a car, bus, etc.	hurl
roam	stravaig
rogue	loon

S

ENGLISH	SCOTTISH
sandwich	piece
scarecrow	tattie-bogle
scared	feart
scatter of coins or sweets to children at a wedding	scrammle
Scottish College of Arms	Lyon Court

Scottish dialect spoken in the north-east	Doric
Scottish School Leaving Certificate	Highers
scream	skreich
scrotum	bawbag
sedate	douce
sex	hochmagandy
shake	shak, shoggle, dirl
shallow drinking cup with two ears	quaich
sharp-tongued person	nippy
sheep or cattle stealer	reiver
shepherd	herd
shining	solasta
shit (*n.*)	keech
shiver (*v.*)	chitter
shoemaker	souter
shoes (typically for sport)	sannies
shriek	skirl, skreich
shy	blate
sicken	scunner
sick-making	bowfin'
simpleton	gowk, tattie-bogle
sing shrilly	skirl
single measure of spirits	nip

slap	skelp (v.)
sleep	kip (n. and v.)
slippers	baffies
slow	blate
sly	pawky
small	peedie, toaty, wee
small child	barra
small, flat-bottomed boat (used for fishing)	coble
small river	burn
small village	clachan
smallholding	croft
smart	canny
smell mouldy	foost
smelly	boggin', howfin'
smoke	reek
smoked haddock	Arbroath smokie
smoky	reekie
sober	douce
soft fluttering	flichterin'
soft woollen bonnet (with a flat circular crown)	tam-o'-shanter
someone or something fantastic	stoater
someone who is making a complete fool of themself	roaster

someone who lives in a city	toonser
sore	sair
speak nonsense	haver
spiced fruit loaf (eaten at New Year)	black bun
spicy food	nippy
spin round	birl (v.)
sportsman's attendant	ghillie
spread thickly	clart
squint-eyed	skelly-eyed
squire	laird
stab	chib
stand someone up	patch
stay	bide
steward	factor
stewed potatoes and other ingredients	stovies
stinging	nippin'
stop	haud
stream	burn
stubborn person	cuddy
students' representative on university court	rector
stupid	glaikit
stupid person	bawheid
stupid, clumsy person	stot

suffer	thole
sunny weather	taps-aff
supporter of Heart of Midlothian FC	Jambo
supreme criminal court, in Edinburgh and circuit towns	High Court of Judiciary
suspect (*v.*)	jalouse
swallow (*v.*)	swally
sweets	snashters

T

ENGLISH	SCOTTISH
tail of a rabbit	fud
talk nonsense	blether (*v.*)
talk of a child	nyaff
tell-tale (*n.*)	clype
term of abuse	bawbag, fud, fannybaws
term of endearment	bastart, brammer, fannybaws, wee barra
term of endearment for a woman	hen

term of endearment for older relatives or friends	big yin
testicles	baws
thick oatmeal cake	bannock
thickly covered	clarted
thin	shilpit
thirsty	drouthy
thrash	wallap
thrashing	laldy
throat	thrapple
throw up	cowk
thump	dunt
tight-fitting	nippit
tiny	toaty
tipstaff	sheriff-officer
tired and bothered	trauchled
to	tae
toilet	cludgie
toilet-head	lavvy heid
too	tae
topsy-turvy	tapsalteerie
totally	pure
tracksuit bottoms	jobby-catchers
trail (v.)	trauchle
tramp	jakey

trinket	whigmaleerie
trouble (*n.*)	fash
troublemaker	ned
trousers	breeks, troosers
turkey	bubbly-jock
turn partly inside out	flype
turnip	neep
twilight	gloamin
two	twa

U

ENGLISH	SCOTTISH
undergo	thole
unhygienic person	mink
upside down	tapsalteerie

V

ENGLISH	SCOTTISH
valley	glen, strath
vault	pend
verger	beadle

very	awfy, deid, pure
vicar in the Episcopal church	rector
vicarage	manse
vulgar	ory

ENGLISH	SCOTTISH
wan	peely-wally
wander	stravaig
wanting rain	routhy
wary	canny
was not	wisnae
water meadow	haugh
weep	greet
well beaten (in sport)	grannied
wet	dreich
wheel along	hurl
who	whae
will	wull
will not	winnae
wily	pawky
wimp	jessie

wooden or metal implement for stirring porridge, etc.	spurtle
woollen cloth with a checked pattern	tartan
worse	waur
would not	wouldnae

ENGLISH	SCOTTISH
yelp of a small dog	nyaff
you	ye
young sea-trout	finnock
young, unmarried woman	quean
younger or shorter person	wee yin
your	yer

SCOTTISH
IDIOMS

SCOTTISH	ENGLISH
a loue ye	I love you
(to take something to) avizandum	to consider a matter
awright ya wee bawbag?	all right, you little scrotum? (a term of endearment)
bide awee	wait a bit
cauld kail hat again	cold cabbage heated up (used figuratively)
come up the Clyde on a banana boat	behave stupidly or naively
dinna fash yersel'	don't bother
dree yer ain wierd	face up to one's destiny
gonny no dae that	please don't do that
hairy coo	highland cow
haste ye back	return soon
haud yer wheesht	stop talking, shut up
he's up tae high doh	flustered

SCOTTISH IDIOMS

SCOTTISH	ENGLISH
I'll gie ye a skelpit lug	I'll give you a slap on the ear
it's a dreich day	it's a cold, damp day
it's just a wheen o' blathers	it's just a pack of nonsense
jings, crivens an' help ma boab!	expression of surprise or admiration, from the comics *Oor Wullie* and *The Broons* by R. D. Low
lang may yer lum reek	long may your chimney smoke
let the tow gang wi' the bucket	let things take their course
oan yer bike	go away
oan yer trolley	go away
och awa' an' dinna talk pish	you're talking a load of rubbish
oot the game	drunk
that's gee-in' me the boak	that's making me feel ill

SCOTTISH	ENGLISH
we're a' Jock Tamson's bairns	we're all the same
whit's fur ye'll no go by ye	what's meant to happen will happen, what will be will be
yer da sells Avon	term of abuse (Avon is a cosmetic brand usually sold by female sales reps)
yer bum's oot the windae	you're not making any sense
yer lookin' a bit peely-wally	you're looking a bit pale

Skinny Malinky Longlegs (n.)

a tall, thin person

Skinny Malinky was a character in a traditional Scottish nursery rhyme that was one of the tenement or 'street' songs sung in playgrounds and urban areas. An article in *The Sunday Times* published in 1956 names Aberdeen as the origin of the song. About a thin man called Skinamalinky Lang Legs, it is still sung as a skipping song today.

PICTURE CREDITS

Shutterstock: Gulf MG, 3; (cow) Tekunidesign, 7; (Forth Bridge) antonpix, 7; DOMSTOCK, 21; Holthoff, 34; Vlada Young, 37; Anton_Ivanov, 55; DesignSpread, 124. Adobe Stock: aksol, 4; Rymden, 67; Elena, 85; AVN Photo Lab, 88. Freepik: rawpixel.com, 13; macrovector, 18; planolla, 25; jemastock, 40; pikisuperstar, 43; macrovector_official, 63; vector_corp, 77; Harryarts, 91. Wikimedia: Nigelcoates, 27; Burn the asylum, 82. thegraphicsfairy.com: 59.